DEREK MAHON

THE YELLOW BOOK

WAKE UNIVERSITY PRESS

Wake Forest University Press. This book is for sale only in North America.
© Derek Mahon and Wake Forest University Press
First U.S. Edition published 1998. Published in association with The Gallery
Press, Loughcrew, Oldcastle, County Meath, Ireland
All rights reserved. For permission, required to reprint or broadcast these
poems, write to: Wake Forest University Press
Post Office Box 7333, Winston-Salem, NC 27109. Printed in the United
States of America. LC card number 97-62511
ISBN 0-916390-82-9 (cloth), ISBN 0-916390-81-0 (paper)

Contents

to the memory of
Eugene Lambe
1939-1994

To live in a decadence need not make us despair; it is but one technical problem the more which a writer has to solve.
— 'Palinurus', *The Unquiet Grave*

Landscape

(after Baudelaire)

Chastely to write these eclogues I need to lie,
like the astrologers, in an attic next the sky
where, high among church spires, I can dream and hear
their grave hymns wind-blown to my ivory tower.
Chin in hand, up here in my apartment block,
I can see workshops full of noise and talk,
cranes and masts of the ocean-going city,
vast cloud formations dreaming about eternity.
I watch a foggy star glitter and shine
in the azure sky, a lamp at a window-pane,
smoke rising into the firmament like incense,
the moon dispensing its mysterious influence.
I watch for spring and summer, autumn too;
and when the winter comes, with silent snow,
I shut the shutters and close the curtains tight
to build my faerie palaces in the night
and dream of love and gardens, blue resorts,
white fountains weeping into marble courts,
birds chirping day and night, whatever notion
excites the infantile imagination . . .
Rattling the window with its riotous squabble
no mob distracts me from my writing-table;
for here I am, up to my usual tricks —
evoking spring-time on the least pretext,
extracting sunlight as my whims require,
my thoughts blazing for want of a real fire.

I

Night Thoughts

One striking post-war phenomenon has been the trans-formation of numerous countries into pseudo-places whose function is simply to entice tourists.
— Paul Fussell, *Abroad*

Night thoughts are best, the ones that visit us
where we lie smoking between three and four
before the first bird and the first tour bus.
Once you would wake up shaking at this hour
but now, this morning, you are a child once more
wide-eyed in an attic room behind the shore
at some generic, gull-pierced seaside town
in war-time Co. Antrim or Co. Down —
navies aglow off Bangor and Whitehead,
dark sea, Glenn Miller's 'Moonlight Serenade',
huge transport planes thundering overhead.
Each white shoe you can remember, each stair-rod,
each streaming window on the Shore Road,
a seaside golf-links on a summer night,
pale sand-dunes stretching away in the moonlight,
'the unbroken crescent of a sandy beach'.
A generation on, these things are here again
while a horse-drawn cab out of the past goes past
toward Leeson St. Night thoughts are best and worst.
My attic window under the shining slates
where the maids slept in the days of Wilde and Yeats
sees crane-light where McAlpine's fusiliers,
site hats and brick-dust, ruin the work of years.
The place a Georgian theme-park for the tourist,
not much remains; though still the first of dawn
whitens a locked park, lilac and hawthorn
dripping in wintry peace, a secret garden

absorbed since the end of summer in its own
patient existence, sea-mist under the trees:
'Wet seats now, water-logged cobwebs everywhere;
believe me, it's all over till next year.'
Soon crocus, daffodil, primrose, the wild bruise
in the iris' eye, and the full watery rose,
those luminous, rain-washed April mornings when
beneath wrought-iron balconies they throng the square,
even in the bathroom I hear them shouting out there —
aliens, space invaders clicking at the front door,
goofy in baseball caps and nylon leisurewear.
. . . Sententious solitude, ancient memory, night
and silence, nobody here; but even as I night-write
blind in a bedside notebook, 'impersonal moonlight
audible on steps, railings, sash window and fanlight',
my biro breaks the silence and something stirs.
Never mind the new world order and the bus tours,
you can still switch on the fire, kick off your shoes
and read the symbolists as the season dies:
Now for the coughing in school dormitories,
the hot drink far from home. November brings
statistics, albums, cocoa, medicine, dreams,
windows flung wide on briny balconies
above an ocean of roofs and lighthouse beams;
like a storm lantern the wintry planet swings.

II

Axel's Castle

A mature artist takes the material closest to hand.
— George Moore

Rain all day; now clouds clear; a brief sun, the winds die;
a wan streak of bilious light in the sky before dark;
'the attic study and the unfinished work' —
Coleridge. Only at dusk Minerva's owl will fly;
only at dusk does wisdom return to the park.
On winter evenings, as the cars flash by,
what hides in there in the kingdom of mould and bark?
Beyond the iron railings and the little gate
only a worm stirs, and dead leaves conflate
in a dried-up fountain crisp-packet and matchbox
(Plato compares a fountain to a flute);
dead leaves up here too, lamplight night and day.
Commuters hustle home to Terenure and Foxrock
while I sit in the inner city with my book
— Petronius, *À Rebours*, *The Picture of Dorian Gray* —
the pleasures of the text, periphrasis and paradox,
some languorous prose at odds with phone and fax.
It's cold up here in the city of litter and drums
while fires glow in the hearths of suburban homes;
I have no peacocks, porphyries, prie-dieu,
no lilies, cephalotis, nepenthes, 'unnatural' vices,
yet I too toil not neither do I spin, I too
have my carefully constructed artificial paradises
and I'm going crazy up here on my own.
I sit here like Domitian in a hecatomb of dead flies,
an armchair explorer in an era of cheap flight
diverted by posters, steamer and sea-plane
at rest in tropical ports. I read where your man
transforms his kitchen into a quarterdeck

to simulate ocean travel and not get sick.
I get sea breezes in my own galley all right,
particularly before dawn when, war in heaven, I hear
remote winds rippling in the stratosphere
and regret never having visited Rio, Shanghai,
Haiti, Singapore or the South Seas; though why
travel when imagination can get you there in a tick
and you're not plagued by the package crowd? A mature
artist takes the material closest to hand;
besides, in our post-modern world economy
one tourist site is much like another site
and the holy city comes down to a Zeno tour,
the closer you get the more it recedes from sight
and the more morons block your vision. Beyond
the back-lit tree-tops of Fitzwilliam Square
a high window is showing one studious light,
somebody sitting late at a desk like me.
There are some die-hards still on the upper floors,
a Byzantine privacy in mews and lane,
but mostly now the famous Georgian doors
will house a junk-film outfit or an advertising agency.
The fountain's flute is silent though time spares
the old beeches with their echoes of Coole demesne;
foreign investment conspires against old decency,
computer talks to computer, machine to answering machine.

III

At the Shelbourne

(Elizabeth Bowen, Nov., 1940)

Sunrise in the Irish Sea, dawn over Dublin Bay
after a stormy night, one shivering star;
and I picture the harsh waking everywhere,
the devastations of a world at war,
airfields, radio silence, a darkened convoy
strung out in moonlight on a glittering sea.
Harsh the wide windows of the hotel at daybreak
as I light up the first ciggie of the day,
stormy the lake like the one in Regent's Park,
glittering the first snow on the Wicklow hills.
Out back, a precipitous glimpse of silent walls,
courtyards, skylights of kitchen and heating plant,
seagulls in rising steam; while at the front
I stand at ease to hear the kettle sing
in an upper room of the Kildare St. wing
admiring the frosty housetops of my birthplace
miraculously immune (almost) to bomb damage.
Sun through south-facing windows lights again
on the oval portrait and the polished surface
where, at an Empire writing-table, I set down
my situation reports for the Dominions Office,
pen-sketches of MacEntee, James Dillon and the rest,
letters to friends in Cork or in Gower St.,
— Virginia, Rosamond and the *Horizon* set —
bright novelistic stuff, a nation on the page:
'. . . *deep, rather futile talks. It is hard afterwards*
to remember the drift, though I remember words,
that smoke-screen use of words! Mostly I meet
the political people; they are very religious.'
There is nothing heroic or 'patriotic' about this;

for here in this rentier heaven of racing chaps,
journalists, cipher clerks, even *Abwehr* types
and talkative day-trippers down from Belfast,
the Mata Hari of the austerity age,
I feel like a traitor spying on my own past.
It was here the ill-fate of cities happened first —
a cruiser in the Liffey, field-guns trained on the GPO,
the kicking-in of doors, dances cancelled, revolvers
served with the morning tea on silver salvers,
a ghostly shipboard existence down below,
people asleep in corridors as now
in the London Underground, mysterious Kôr,
a change of uniforms in the cocktail bar
though the bronze slave-girls still stand where they were,
Nubian in aspect, in manner art-nouveau.
I must get the Austin out of the garage,
drive down this week-end to Bowen's Court
if I can find petrol, and back for the Sunday mail-boat —
though this is home really, a place of warmth and light,
a house of artifice neither here nor there
between the patrician past and the egalitarian future,
tempting one always to prolong one's visit:
in war, peace, rain or fog you couldn't miss it
however late the hour, however dark the night.

IV

'shiver in your tenement'

I load myself with chains and try to get out of them.
— Austin Clarke

You might have thought them mature student, clerk
or priest once, long ago in the demure '60s
before the country first discovered sex —
Cathal O'Shannon, Harry Kernoff, Austin Clarke
arriving by bus at noon in search of roguery
from Howth, Raheny, Monkstown or Templeogue,
some house by bridge or woodland *à l'usage*
of the temporal, of the satiric or lyric Muse.
Gravely they strolled down Dawson or Grafton St.,
thoughtful figures amid the faces, the laughter,
or sat among the race-goers and scroungers
in Sinnot's, Neary's, the Bailey, the Wicklow Lounge —
pale, introspective almost to the point of blindness
or so it seemed, living the life of the mind,
of European *littérateurs*, their black Quartier hats
(all purchased from the same clerical outfitter)
suggestive of first editions and dusty attics.
They sipped watery Jameson — without ice, of course —
knew London and Paris but preferred the unforced
pace of the quiet city under the Dublin mountains
where a broadsheet or a broadcast might still count.
Those were the days before tourism and economic growth,
before deconstruction and the death of the author,
when pubs had as yet no pictures of Yeats and Joyce
since people could still recall their faces, their voices;
of crozier-wielding bishops, vigilant censors,
pre-Conciliar Latin, smoke pouring from swung censers;
of sexual guilt, before French letter and Dutch cap,
fear muttered in the dark of dormitory and side-chapel.

There was much dark then in the archdiocese
though some, like you, had found a gap of brightness.
Now, of course, we live in a blaze of tropical light
under a green pagoda sunshade globally warm
like the slick glass on a renovated farmhouse.
Mnemosyne, mother of nine, dust at St. Patrick's,
labour 'accustomed to higher living', poverty old hat,
does art benefit from the new dispensation?
What, in our new freedom, have we left to say?
Oh, poets can eat now, painters can buy paint
but have we nobler poetry, happier painting
than when the gutters bubbled, the drains stank
and hearts bobbed to the clappers in the sanctuary?
Has art, like life itself, its source in agony?
Nothing to lose but our chains, our chains gone
that bound with form the psycho-sexual turbulence,
together with those black hats and proper pubs,
at home now with the ersatz, the pop, the phony,
we seldom see a real nun, a copy of *An Phoblacht*
or love and hate, as once, with a full heart.
Those were the days; now patience, courage, artistry,
solitude things of the past, like the fear of God,
we nod to you from the pastiche paradise of the post-modern.

V

Schopenhauer's Day

I am all these things, and besides me there is nothing.
— Upanishads

What does the old bastard see when he looks down?
A creature of habit like everyone in this town,
he has lived up there above the promenade
for more than twenty years, and every day
observed the same deliberate formulae
now second nature: up at dawn, just one
mug of his favourite Java before work
— mind-body problems — flute practice (K.299),
the Pan-pipes in honour of a previous life;
then lunch with students at the Englischer Hof
and reads till four, when he goes for the daily walk —
two hours, neither more nor less, hail, rain or shine.
At six to the library and a magazine,
a thicket of fiddle-bows in the Kaisersaal,
a solitary supper at the Stork Hotel,
home by ten and early to bed: a protocol
perfected over the years and one designed
to release from trivia the aspiring mind.
Cabs and coaches bump and shove in the square,
the money-making craze is everywhere;
but a fire of pine or spruce keeps out the cold.
A mildly valetudinarian bachelor,
he stares from the window at his idea of the world,
its things-in-themselves, the sun rising once more
on bridge and embankment, baroque edifice, Gothic spire,
freight barges cracking ice down to the Rhine
and the innocent flower-gardens of the south shore
beaming with self-delight, churning with worms:
the earth and he were never on intimate terms.

Minerals rage, base metals dreaming of gold
in the hills, while St. Bartholomew chimes the hour;
plants, water, citizens, the very stone
expand with a sulphurous purpose of their own,
the very viruses scream to the higher forms.
Tat tvam asi; these living things we are
but only in the extinction of our desire,
absorption of the knower in the known.
There are perceptual difficulties, the *trompe-l'oeil*
of virtual reality; for what is real really?
Often we think what we see is not what we think we see;
he too is a mere appearance dreamt by another system,
he can't get through to the world nor the world to him.
As the Buddhists do, he tries to concentrate
on a faint chime (say) or on the idea of 'white'
while knowing these exercises cannot mitigate
life's guilt or the servitude of love and hate.
The only solution lies in *art for its own sake*,
redemption through the aesthetic, as birds in spring
sing for their own delight, even if they also sing
from physical need; it comes to the same thing.
'No rose without a thorn, many a thorn without a rose.'
Bring out the poets and the artists; take
music, the panacea for all our woes,
the heartfelt calculus of Mozart
or the calm light of Dutch interior art;
and yet, he says, he fears for the fate of those
born in a later era, as if our bleak
and pitiless whoring after the sublime,
implying conflict as sublimity does,
bequeathed some frightfulness to a future time:
'Through the cortex a great melancholy blows
as if I'd seen the future in a dream —
Weimar, a foul Reich and the days of wrath,
a *Vogue* model in the dead dictator's bath;

angels of history, boisterous young men
coming in planes when we are dead and gone
to make the cities a rubble of ash and bone
while black soldiers tap-dance on my gravestone.'

VI

To Eugene Lambe in Heaven

— University Rd., Belfast, 1961; etc.

It's after closing-time on a winter's night
in Smokey Joe's café a generation ago —
rain and smoke, and the tables are packed tight
with drunken students kicking up a racket,
exchanging insults, looking for a fight
since there's nothing to do and nowhere else to go;
and the sad Italians (parents, daughter, son)
who own the place and serve these savages
of the harsh north their chips and sausages
look up and grin with relief as you come in,
their baffled faces lighting up at once
at your quaint 'whisker' and velvet smoking-jacket,
your manner that of an exiled Stuart prince
transfiguring tedium . . . Next year you appeared
in the same gear and spread Tolstoyan beard,
our ginger man, in Trinity's front square
you called the 'playground' once; and it was here
in pub and flat you formed the character
we came to love, colloquial yet ornate,
one of those perfect writers who never write,
a student of manners and conversation straight
from the pages of Castiglione or Baudelaire:
'a form of pride rare in this generation,
stoical, spiritual even, resistant to the trite;
the Protestant countries lack gallantry and devotion . . .'
Not that you read much, you had no need to read
so flunked your courses; destined for the law
took up, instead, interior decoration,
installing yourself wherever the calling led
and awaiting the 'crock of gold' you never saw.

23

Thus on a summer evening you might be found,
older even than the rugs you sat among,
an indolent perfectionist on a chaise-longue
in some fine house, the property of a friend,
a citrous gin or herbal tea to hand,
young women in attendance, an abashed host constrained
to listen patiently while you explained
the iniquity of ownership; for you had no ambition
save for the moment, of will-power not a whit
since nothing could measure up to your idea of it.
Dublin in the '60s! — Golden days
with Clarke making a comeback, Kavanagh in his final phase;
then London, Covent Garden, quit the booze
but dreamed the hashish poem on opera nights,
De Quincey's 'infinite ecstasies, infinite repose'
while living above the market unknown to the old fogies
ensconced in the Garrick with their port and stogies
and the hacks in the Coach & Horses, *laudatores*
temporis acti, unregenerate Tories
shut out for ever from your generous insights.
At a time of drag and Pop Art, hair and clothes,
Beardsley prints, floral design and rainbow hues,
of Quant and Biba, Shrimpton and Twiggy, lurid tights,
gratuitous gesture, instant celebrity, insolent pose,
yours was a sociable life but a lonely one,
your castle of indolence a monastic den
where you could smoke late and contemplate the din
of Leicester Square, Long Acre and Drury Lane,
vocations entertained but never followed through.
A job, a house, a car, perhaps a wife,
financial panic, the 'normal' sort of life
so many know, such things were not for you
who made the great refusal but remained
philosophical with your dwindling flow of visitors,
chivalrous with women, ceremonious with waiters,

24

noble in exile, tragic in the end,
and died dancing . . . But hip went out of fashion
in an age of sado-monetarism; and the game
now is to the 'oeconomists and calculators' —
the new harshness must have wounded you to the heart.
We always knew you had too big a heart,
we always knew about the heart condition
you nursed with a vegetarian regime
of rice and nuts. You were a saint and hero
to the young men and girls we used to know
once in the golden age; and now it's closing-time
in the condemned playgrounds that you loved, Eugene,
in Davy Byrne's and Smokey Joe's. The scene
is draggy now in these final days, and with
everyone famous for fifteen minutes, few
will survive except those, like you, the stuff of myth.
Oft in the stilly night I remember our wasted youth.

VII

An Bonnán Buí

A heron-like species, rare visitors, most recent records
referring to winter months . . . very active at dusk.
— Guide to Irish Birds

A sobering thought, the idea of you stretched there,
bittern, under a dark sky, your exposed bones
yellow too in a ditch among cold stones,
ice glittering everywhere on bog and river,
the whole unfortunate country frozen over
and your voice stilled by enforced sobriety —
a thought more wrenching than the fall of Troy
because more intimate; for we'd hear your shout
of delight from a pale patch of watery sunlight
out on the mud there as you took your first
drink of the day and now, destroyed by thirst,
you lie in brambles while the rats rotate.
I'd've broken the ice for you, given an inkling;
now, had I known the score, we might both be drinking
and singing too; for mine is the same story.
Others have perished — heron, blackbird, thrushes —
and lie shivering like you under whin-bushes;
but I mourn only the bittern, withdrawn and solitary,
a highbrow with a hunched gait and quick forensic eye
who used to carouse alone among the rushes
and sleep rough in the star-glimmering bog-drain.
It used to be, with characters like us,
they'd let us wander the roads in wind and rain
or lock us up and throw away the key;
but now they have a cure for these psychoses
as indeed they do for most social diseases.
At peace in my patch of sunlit convalescence
with vitamin pills and a bottle of mineral water,

forced on the dry too, should I not be bitter?
What do psychiatrists *want*? — An age of prose;
except for Anthony Clare, a 'shrewd repose',
a world-clinic where the odd learn to renounce
their singularity for a more communal faith,
the coward 'survives his self-inflicted death',
we step out into the light, seal up the door
of the torture chamber and the ivory tower
and, like the man said, study war no more;
for ours is an age of reflection, circumspection,
a time for grief-work and polite sex.
And the lyrical madness? If no saint or hero,
no goddess 'all saints and sober men' revile;
no music without hunger, can we still expect
to know the Muses' wicked, intolerant smile?
No dope, no 'Kubla Khan'; no schizophrenia, no *Chimères*,
do we love one another and build the shining city
renouncing the sublime for a quieter beauty
or fight to the death about the nature of reality?
Do we want the Renascence art-and-poison paradox
or a thousand years of chocolate and cuckoo clocks?
Do we choose peace to please some foreign power,
war-like itself elsewhere, or do we prefer
the intransigence, bittern, of our native Ulster,
the bigots shrieking for their beleaguered 'culture'?
Do we give up fighting so the tourists come
or fight the harder so they stay at home?
Waving and drowning, the restored spirit floats
in blue water, the rising tide that lifts some boats.

VIII

Remembering the '90s

Beyond the light stand failure and remorse . . .
— Philip Larkin, *High Windows*

The snow-man infants from the nursery school
devised from the first fall of January
stares back from a far corner of the square —
a selfish giant made to freeze and rule
the garden as if self-generated there,
his abstract mien and cold, bituminous eye
proclaiming a different order of reality
from the bright children who gave rise to him.
When they go there to play at mid-morning
their primary colours seem to prefigure spring,
the deliquescence of each rigorous thing;
but the ex-child at the window watching them,
specs on his nose and winter in his eyes,
knows himself outcast from the continuum
and draws his curtain against darkening skies . . .
A long time since the hearties and the aesthetes,
imperious questors and saint-faced degenerates,
old boys of Yeats's 'tragic' (pathetic) generation
in cricketing blazers and inept bow-ties
who ate the altar rails, pawned pride for drinks,
who died of thirst *auprès de la fontaine*
or tumbled from high stools in the Rose & Crown.
Those desperate characters of the previous '90s,
slaves of the Siren, consorts of the Sphinx
like Dowson, Johnson, Symons and Le Gallienne
were heroes, though, compared with our protagonist,
a decadent who lived to tell the story,
surviving even beyond the age of irony
to the point where the old stuff comes round again;

and this is the sin against the Holy Ghost,
the cynicism that views with equanimity
the enemies of promise, *les amours jaunes*,
the organism dark with booze and nicotine.
'Today is the first day of the rest of your life'?
— tell that to your liver; tell that to your ex-wife.
Owning like them 'an indolent, restless gift',
fitful, factitious and at best makeshift,
burning without warmth or illumination,
each verse co-terminous with its occasion,
each line the pretext for a precious cadence,
I keep alight the cold candle of decadence.
A rueful veteran of the gender wars,
in 'the star-crowned solitude of [mine] oblivious hours'
I remember London twilights blue with gin
sub regno Cynarae, the wine and roses
where 'She-who-must-be-obeyed', furs next the skin,
drove us to celibacy or satyriasis:
forgive me, love, for my apostasies.
'Nothing, of course, not even conventional virtue
is so provincial as conventional vice'
— Symons, *The Symbolist Movement in Literature*.
The most of what we did and wrote was artifice,
rhyme-sculpture against the entangling vines of nature —
a futile project since, in the known future,
new books will be rarities in techno-culture,
a forest of intertextuality like this,
each one a rare book and what few we have
written for prize-money and not for love,
while the *real* books like vintage wines survive
among the antiquities, each yellowing page
known only to astrologer and mage
where blind librarians study as on a keyboard
gnomic encryptions, secrets of the word,
a lost knowledge; and all the rest is lit(t)erature.

IX

At the Gate Theatre

There are no longer protagonists; there is only the chorus.
— Ortega y Gasset

Now the story of Phèdre *is very well known, but perhaps
the story of the* Bacchae *is not so well known.*
— Stevie Smith,
Novel on Yellow Paper

(for Dearbhla Molloy)

'. . . Ah, what new pain must I now undergo?
What monstrous torture have I yet to know?
All I've endured, the madness and the fear,
self-pity, rage, humiliation, self-hate,
the insult of rejection, even, were mere
ripples of the approaching storm . . . ' Not many
in the trade now can decently impersonate
the great ones of the tragic repertoire
— Medea, Cleopatra, Gruoch Macbeth —
much less achieve the famous 'diamond edge'
of the doomed Phaedra's lightning-inviting rage,
her great apostrophes to love and death;
so here I am, like any stage-door Johnny,
with a bunch of irises and a bottle of Moët
to call your playing-out of Phaedra's agony,
your bright contralto, stringed and star-lit vertigo
of outrage and despair from head to toe
not only wonderful but actually sublime
in the old sense of resistance overcome,
articulate terror, storm answered with storm,
a heaven-splitting performance. When she cries
defiance to the gods, the wings, the quivering flies,

we know we are in the presence; but we know too
a whole theatrical tradition is in crisis —
this play peaked and exhausted all at once
an entire genre; for its fierce eloquence
yielded in no time to the *comic* Muse,
the death of tragedy and the birth of the blues.
Backstage tonight, I glimpse the ghostly faces
of Micheál and Hilton, Geraldine and Siobhán,
the Hamlets and the Heddas, Dorians and Salomés
amid the festive racket of make-up and paint-sprays,
moonlit revels and laughter in the dark,
the thrill of envenom'd chalice and poisonous book;
for tragedy too, of course, is enormous fun
though now we've no use for the tragic posture.
When the mad queen conducts her futile strife
with the blank forces of inhospitable nature
we see that the problem is not death but life —
the only cure for tragedy, the one sure
antibiotic against original sin. In the early days
the Greeks followed tragedies with satyr plays;
and look at the old age of Euripides
who, after a lifetime struggling with new ideas,
sent out his Bacchae to the woods and glens
to dance devotion to the god of vines
under the rocks, under the moonlit pines.
Bring on ivy and goatskin, pipe and drum,
for Dionysus son of Semele is come
to tell us our long servitude to the sublime
is over, no further resistance offered by the medium,
the whole history of creative tension a waste of time.
Goodbye now to 'the tragic sense of life',
all we want is a soap serial and a dirty laugh
who have had our fill of horrors and prefer a rock
opera or a midsummer night's sex comedy
to the death of kings. Bring on the new regime

of airy shapes, nothings, fluff and bubbles, 'holiday'
where the white light of physics yields to the dark
garden of dance and dream and here comes everybody
to celebrate midsummer with a rave and a riot,
to mate with fluting satyrs, fornicate
with donkeys, or with a monster fall in love.
— *What night-rule now about this haunted grove?*

X

The Idiocy of Human Aspiration

(Juvenal, *Satires*, X)

. . . but great wealth is the worst. Who'd want to be
a big fish gobbling up the smaller fry
when it's the big fish who attract hostility
like Seneca and the rest in Nero's day?
You're better off to sit tight in your room,
take change if you go out walking after dark
and keep your wits about you in the park
where a knife gleams behind each shadowy tree.
All pursue riches in our modern Rome,
gardens, a coach-house and a stately home;
but poison's seldom served in wooden cups —
beware the crystal glass and golden bowl,
be careful when you raise wine to your lips.
Which of the philosophers shall we extol,
the one who, standing on his front steps,
smiles, or the one who weeps? Easy to smile,
if we started weeping there'd be no end to it.
Democritus would shake with continual mirth,
even in *his* primitive times, at life on earth
and showed that stoicism spiced up with wit,
some candour and good sense, can dissipate
even the thick air of a provincial city.
All anyone does now is fuck and shit;
instant gratification, 'entertainment', longevity
we ask, but mumbling age comes even so —
the striking profile thick and stricken now,
the drooping member like a broken bough,
the simian features and the impatient heir.
What else can you expect from your white hair,
your voice like cinders under a kitchen door?

33

What use to you the glittering *décolletages*,
the best box in the house above the stage,
when you are blind and deaf? Now fever and disease
run rampant through our waste anatomies,
the old mind dithering in its anecdotage,
the joints all seizing up with rheumatism,
seek guidance of the heavenly gods who treasure
our lives more than we do ourselves. Subdued
by protocol and the fear of solitude,
you wed in haste and now repent at leisure
even as your hands shake in their final spasm.
Ask for a sound mind in a sound body
unfrightened of the grave and not demented
by grief at natural declension; study
acceptance in the face of fate; and if
you want to worship mere materialism,
that modern god we have ourselves invented,
I leave you to the delights of modern life.

XI

At the Chelsea Arts Club

Everything aspires to the condition of rock music.
Besieged by Shit, Sperm, Garbage, Gristle, Scum
and other 'raucous trivia', we take refuge
from fan migrations, police presence, road rage,
narcotics, Abrakebabra, festive rowdytum,
from Mick and Gazza, Hugh Grant, paparazzi,
TOP TORIES USED ME AS THEIR SEX TOY
and Union-jacquerie at its most basic
in shadowy, murmurous citadels like this
beside Whistler's Thames, once 'clothed in evening mist
where the buildings lose themselves in a dim sky,
the great chimneys become campanili
and warehouses are palaces in the night'.
Now both embankments gleam with exhausted chrome
grumbling at funeral pace, with the home team
up in the league and quoted on the exchange
and interest in the game at fever pitch,
we treasure the more those symphonies in white,
those nocturnes consecrating wharf and bridge.
Elsewhere the body art, snuff sculpture, trash aesthetics,
the video nasties and shock computer graphics;
but here you still might meet with 'significant form' —
indeed, the interior illustrates the term
with its retro mode and billiard table, piano,
'the whole place rather like a studio',
shirts by Jekyll & Hyde, the wine and roses,
the sniftery dandies at their studied poses,
the eyepatch woman and the monocle man,
garden and sky rose-red and Dufy-blue.
Maybe I'm finally turning into an old fart
but I do prefer the traditional kinds of art,
respect for materials, draughtsmanship and so on —

though I'm in two minds about Tank Girl over there,
the Muse in chains, a screw-bolt in one ear,
the knickers worn over the biking gear . . .
Best in the afternoon when the bar is shut,
the smoking room, an empty Chekhov set,
stained ochre, yields to silence, buttery light,
euphoria and nostalgia; so let me write
in praise of yellow while it is still bright,
of crocus and freesia, primrose and daffodil,
the novels of Huxley, Rimbaud's missing vowel,
yahoos, yippies, yuppies, yoga, yoghurt, Yale,
apricot and tangerine, baby clothes and toys,
prohibition, quarantine, caution, cowardice, buoys,
lamplight, gaslight, candlelight, illness, fog,
pencils, *I Ching*, golf, Roman fever, bubonic plague,
illuminated scripture, Klimt and Schiele, Kafka's Prague,
Aladdin's lamp and genie, mechanical earth-movers,
treason, deceit, infection, misery, unhappy lovers,
a night wake, magic realism, Gnosticism, Cabbalism,
guilt and grief, conspiracy theories, crime,
the back pages, dangerous liaisons, journalism,
charity, sunlit smoke, delight and shame,
angels and archangels, cherubim and seraphim,
the earliest buses, the Congo, Manhattan taxis,
cottage doors, the old *telefón* boxes,
failure, the word 'curious', the word 'screech'
and the little patch of brick Swann liked so much.

XII

Aphrodite's Pool

I dive and rise in an explosion of spindrift
and drift to a turtle-faced inflatable raft —
evening, Cyclades, one cloud in the azure,
a brain-scan light-show swarming on blue tiles,
a flickering network of vague energies
as on dolphin murals and docked caique bows,
a murmuring hosepipe where the pool fills,
snatches of music from a quiet house,
the wash-house like a temple to the Muses;
on a marble slab flipper and apple core,
straw hat and wristwatch in a deckchair,
sandal and white sock. Nymphs have been here;
water nymphs have been here printing the blind
nap-time silence with supernatural toes
and casting magic on the ruffled water
still agitated by a dry seasonal wind.
A last plane fades beyond the glittering sound,
its wild surf-boards and somnolent fishing-boats,
as the air fills with cicadas and mosquitoes,
the sky with sunset and astronomy; goats
and donkeys nod in the god-familiar hills
among spaceship vertebrae and white asphodels.
The prone body is mine, that of a satyr,
a fat, unbronzed, incongruous visitor
under the fairy lights and paper frills
of a birthday party I was too late to attend.
Aloof from the disco ships and buzzing bikes
the pool ticks faintly among quiet rocks;
rose petals on the surface and in the air,
mimosa and jasmine fragrance everywhere,
I flirt like some corrupt, capricious emperor
with insects dithering on the rim; for this

is the mythic moment of metamorphosis
when quantitative becomes qualitative and genes
perform their atom-dance of mad mutation . . .
I climb out, shower off chlorine and sun-lotion,
and a hot turquoise underwater light
glows like Atlantis in the Aegean night;
network, stars-of-the-sea, perpetual motion,
a star-net hums in the aphrodisiac sea-lanes.

XIII

Dusk

(*after Baudelaire*)

Night now, bewitching night, friend of the evil-doer,
sneaks up like an accomplice; like a boudoir
the sky closes; and men, mild in themselves,
change into ravening vampires and werewolves.
Soft night, desired by the unfortunate ones
whose limbs articulate with aches and groans
a day of servitude; night that relieves
those victims sacrificed to arduous lives —
the driven thinker with his ashen face,
the cleaning-woman who can know release.
Unwholesome spirits in the atmosphere
wake stupidly, meanwhile, like businessmen
and, cruising bat-like through the evening air,
flap at the door-post and the window-pane.
Under the lamplight that the wind teases
the whores light up outside the whorehouses
like ants pouring out of their black holes;
insurgents waiting for the word to strike,
they fan out everywhere through dark defiles
in diseased organs of the body politic
like flies that buzz around an open sewer.
You can hear a kitchen whistle here and there,
a playhouse laugh, a concert thump and blare;
restaurants loud with the uproar of card-games
fill up with pimps and pushers, their good chums,
and thieves who neither rest nor pity know
will soon be at their dirty business too,
privily forcing bureau drawer and strong-box
to stuff their face and clothe their mistress' backs.
Be still, my soul, at this unearthly hour

and stop your ears to its incessant roar,
for now the sufferings of the sick increase.
Night takes them by the throat; their struggles cease
as one by one they head for the great gulf;
the wards fill with their cries, who soon enough
will come no more to sup the fragrant broth
with a loved one, at dusk, by a known hearth —
for some of us have never known the relief
of house and home, being outcast in this life.

XIV

Rue des Beaux-Arts

*There is only one thing . . . worse than being talked
about, and that is not being talked about.*
— Oscar Wilde,
The Picture of Dorian Gray

The new art is everywhere with its whiplash line
derived from pre-Raff ivy and twining vine,
its biomorphic shapes, motifs of cat and moth;
base metals and industrial design,
outside and inside, in themselves uncouth,
aspire to the carnal life of pond and bower —
and you yourself, old trendy that you are,
have exchanged the silvery tinkle of champagne
for muddy clouds of absinthe and vermouth,
bitter herbs self-prescribed to make you whole.
As you said, a yellow-journalism survivor
has no need to fear the yellow fever;
but it's mid-July and nature has crept back
to the rue des Beaux-Arts and the rue du Bac,
the humid side-streets of the Latin quarter
with its rank plants and warm municipal water,
its fiery pavements scorching feet and soul;
'the whole body gives out a silent scream'.
A man of griefs, acquainted with insomnia,
you doze most of the day with curtains drawn
against the hot-house light of afternoon,
rising at agate Paris dusk to take
your walk by the twilit river, *quai des brumes*,
visit a church to chew the altar rail
(what ever happened to the Greek ideal?)
and check with the sales people at Galignani's
on the latest magazines; and more than once

you've mixed with tourists in the Luxembourg
to watch schoolchildren under the stony gaze
of Anne de Bretagne and Marguerite de Provence
and listen to infants piping in the Coupole,
your Babylonian features raised in reminiscence.
'Art's mainspring, the love of life, is gone;
prose is so much more difficult.' The morgue
yawns, as it yawned too for Verlaine, Laforgue,
nor will you see your wife and sons again.
Gestures, a broken series; performance strain;
judge by appearances and what you get
is an old windbag. Still full of hot air,
still queer as fuck and putting on the style,
you spout in the Odéon given half a chance
for yours is the nonchalance of complete despair.
'The thing now is to forget him; let him go
to that limbo of oblivion which is his due' —
though the *Daily Chronicle* and the *St. James' Gazette*
are gone, while you are talked of even yet.
Back-lit by sunset, a great trench of sky
glows like a brazier; grotesque tableaux,
unprecedented animals are engraved there
in angelic purple-and-gold photography
and the stars shine like oil-lamps. Gazing west
you can just make out the tip of Finistère
where the last rock explodes in glistening mist.
'They will not want me again in airy mood;
they would like me to edit prayers for those at sea.'
Job with a skin-rash and an infected ear,
Oisín in the real world of enforced humility,
you pine still for the right kind of solitude
and the right kind of society; but it's too late
to benefit from the astringency of the sea
or come to terms with the nature you pooh-poohed;
for you, if anyone, have played your part

42

constraining nature in the name of art,
surviving long enough for the birth-knell
of a new century and a different world.
Go sup with the dead, the party's life and soul:
'The greatest men fail, or seem to have failed.'

XV

Smoke

Bone-idle, I lie listening to the rain,
not tragic now nor yet 'to frenzy bold' —
must I stand out in thunder yet again
who have *thrice* come in from the cold? Sold
on sobriety, I turn to the idea of nicotine,
my opium, hashish, morphine and cocaine,
'Turkish on the left, Virginia on the right',
my cigarette a lighthouse in the night.
Autumn in Dublin; safe home from New York,
I climb as directed to our proper dark,
five flights without a lift up to the old
gloom we used to love, and the old cold.
Head in the clouds but tired of verse, I fold
away my wind-harp and my dejection odes
and mute the volume on the familiar phone
('. . . leave your number; speak after the tone')
to concentrate on pipe-dreams and smoke-clouds.
Skywards smoke from my last Camel rises
as elsewhere from our natural resources
and the contagious bonfire of the vanities
like pillars of cloud. I was with Xenophon
in Persia, I was with the conquistadors
when first they landed on American shores
in search of a trade-route to the Orient
and found instead, to their bewilderment,
a sot-weed continent in the western ocean.
Now closing-time and the usual commotion,
crowds and cars as if to a revolution . . .
Blue in the face behind my veils of smoke
I try to recapture pool dreams or evoke
aesthetic rapture, images of felicity,
the mist on Monet's nebulous nenuphars

or the dawn vision of a subsiding city
'rising like water-columns from the sea',
everyone crowding to the rail to see
the Tiepolo frescoes in the Gesuati,
clouds of glory, Elysian yellows and blues.
We are all tourists now and there is no escape;
smoke gets in your face, in your eyes, up your nose
but offers inspiration, aspiration, hope,
chimeras, ghosts, 'pure speculative ether',
an a-political sphere above the weather.
26. INT. RICK'S. A night-club, expensive, chic
with an air of sophistication and intrigue
and everybody puffing, those were the days
of legendary nuance, 'drift', lavender haze.
No puffing now, not even on Death Row,
even in the electric chair tobacco is taboo.
The last addicts gather at the last strand
for a last smoke-out on the burning sand
with Ekberg, Warhol, Guevara, Bowen and Cocteau,
ashes to ashes at the rainbow's end —
we are under a cloud, our world gone with the wind.
. . . What *use* is it, you ask, as we exhale
clouds of unknowing with our last gasp. Well,
it suggests alternatives to the world we know
and is to that extent consoling; also
'a man should have an occupation of some kind'.
Raleigh, for instance, spent his time in Youghal
weighing cigars against cigar ashes to find
the weight of smoke, perhaps even of the soul;
and Bakhtin under siege, no soap, no supper,
used his own manuscripts as cigarette paper.

XVI

America Deserta

(postscript to 'The Hudson Letter')

> *High in the air float green-blue copper roofs*
> *like the tips of castles rising from the clouds*
> *in fairy tales and cigarette advertisements.*
> — Zelda Fitzgerald,
> *Harper's Bazaar*, 1929

Often enough you've listened to me complain
of the routine sunlight and infrequent rain
beyond the ocean blue; and now, begod,
where once it never drizzled but it poured,
in dirty Dublin and even in grim Belfast
our cherished rainfall is a thing of the past,
our climate now that of the world at large
in the post-Cold War, global-warming age
of corporate rule, McPeace and Mickey Mao.
Imitative in all things, we mimic now,
as nature art, the general new-age weather,
a smiley-face of glib promotional blather;
anxious not to be left behind, we seize
on the dumb theory and the prescribed disease
who were known once for witty independence
and valued things beyond the world of sense;
subscribing eagerly to the post-modern kitsch
we shirk our noble birthright as the glitch
in the internet, the thorn in the side, the pain
in the neck and the (holy) ghost in the machine.
An alien among aliens during my New York time
spying for the old world in the new, thought-crime
grown secretly like a window-box of cannabis
in the shocking privacy of a book-lined space,

I valued above all our restful evening walks
to the West Side pierheads and the desolate docks
under a sunset close-encounter blaze
to watch the future form from the heat-haze
in the garbage-mouth of the Hudson. We never hung
with the fast cocaine crowd or the surfing young
but glimpsed from cloudy dirigible heights
the neon-fingered dawns and laser nights,
knew leaves 'show-cased' in ice, the 'sick' limo,
the virtual park and lamp-post in the snow,
those retro scenes beloved of Sam Menashe
and the hard-drinking, chain-smoking Eurotrash —
an older America of the abrasive spirit,
film noir, real jazz and grown-up literate wit.
Even then, though, life was imitating art
with palaces in the air, each one a fort
in a mediaeval city gripped by plague —
a nightmare, said Neruda, of 'corruption and fatigue',
mergers and acquisitions, leveraged buy-outs, corporate raiding,
'casino manifestations in program and index trading' . . .
Back home, I surf the bright box for world news
and watch with sanctimonious European eyes
the continuing slave narrative, people in chains,
the limp ship firing into the vegetation,
stick children, tanks, where once again warplanes
emerge from rain-clouds with a purposeful growl
as in the depths of Nostradamus' midnight water-bowl;
drought, famine, genocide, frustrated revolution
and the silent roar of 'ant-like' migration,
all this to serve discredited ambition
and the pages of *Vanity Fair* and *Harper's Bazaar*.
Not long from barbarism to decadence, not far
from liberal republic to defoliant empire
and thence to entropy; not long before
the pharaonic scam begins its long decline

to pot-holed roads and unfinished construction sites,
as in the 'dark' ages a few scattered lights —
though it's only right and proper we set down
that in our time New York was a lot of fun.
I think of diner mornings in ice and thaw,
the Lion's Head, renamed the Monkey's Paw,
and moments on the Hudson River Line;
you wildly decadent in forbidden furs
in the shadow of the Bobst or the Twin Towers,
the skyline at your back, the pearl-rope bridges
and a nation singing its heart out in the business pages.

XVII

The World of J. G. Farrell

It was, after all, only the lack of perspective that made it seem he would be swept away.

(*for Lavinia Greacen*)

A huge house (*Troubles*) at the water's edge
whistling and groaning in the wind from the sea,
blind windows, flying slates, whole days of reverie,
'the cemetery of all initiative and endeavour',
outbuildings, tea-gold streams, a heathery road,
a yellow vintage 'motor' in the garage,
crows bickering high up in a foggy wood,
vegetable encroachments, intestinal shapes,
the click and ripple of exhausted pipes,
a creeper twining around a naked light
while a young man, inspected by binoculars,
harangues a restive crowd from a watery rock;
hill stations deserted (*Siege*), impenetrable foliage,
long bars empty (*Grip*) in tropical heat,
their pools afloat with matchboxes and driftwood,
fly-blown verandahs, ceiling fans at rest,
carnivorous plants entangling gates and fences,
the coercive empire an empire of the senses,
of rustling organisms and whispering rain-forest,
a dripping silence after torrential rain,
the fluttering butterfly that starts the hurricane.
Whisper, immortal Muse, of the insanity of the great,
the futility of control, the proximity of the pit,
of babies in the dust, smoking rubbish, a circling kite.
The girls from Goa, in silk and satin and boa,
have boarded the last ship out of the opium war
while Gurkha riflemen parade at the aerodrome

to a skirl of bagpipes and the 'Skye Boat Song'
leaving to the Chinese, if they so desire,
the investment banks and polo fields of Hong Kong,
the Coke and Marlboro ads; they're going home.
Everyone's going home now, those with homes to go to;
the bugles blow and the Union Jack comes down
in the West Indies and the Antarctic soon,
Bermuda, Antigua, South Georgia and Pitcairn
and even, who knows, Gibraltar and Ulster too.
The big-game trophies and lion skins have gone
from the cold interiors of northern Europe
while the consular derelict with his jungle juice
and perpendicular terror of the abyss
can take the cure and start to live in hope.
Better a quiet life, the moon in a bucket of water
with nobody there to hear though the stars do
and a bedside book like the teachings of Chuang Tzu —
type of the unselfconscious thinker who,
never a slave to objective reality, knew
the identity of contraries, traced us from the germ
and saw our vital unity with the rest of nature;
disdained, of course, utilitarian system;
like Echo, answered only when called upon
in bamboo cage or palace of white jade.
We have lost our equilibrium, he said;
gaze at the world but leave the world alone.
Do nothing; do nothing and everything will be done.

XVIII

Death in Bangor

We stand — not many of us — in a new cemetery
on a cold hillside in the north of Co. Down
staring at an open grave or out to sea,
the lough half-hidden by great drifts of rain.
Only a few months since you were snug at home
in a bungalow glow, keeping provincial time
in the chimney corner, *News-Letter* and *Woman's Own*
on your knee, wool-gathering by Plato's firelight,
a grudging flicker of flame on anthracite.
Inactive since your husband died, your chief
concern the 'appearances' that ruled your life
in a neighbourhood of bay windows and stiff
gardens shivering in the salt sea air,
the rising-sun motif on door and gate,
you knew the secret history of needlework,
bread-bin and laundry basket awash with light,
the straight-backed chairs, the madly chiming clock.
The figure in the *Republic* returns to the cave,
a Dutch interior where cloud-shadows move,
to examine the intimate spaces, chest and drawer,
the lavender in the linen, the savings book,
the kitchen table silent with nobody there.
Shall we say the patience of an angel? No,
not unless angels be thought anxious too
and God knows you had reason to be; for yours
was an anxious time of nylon and bakelite,
market-driven hysteria on every fretwork radio,
your frantic kitsch decor designed for you
by thick industrialists and twisted ministers
('Nature's a bad example to simple folk'); and yet
with your wise monkeys and euphemistic 'Dresden' figurines,
your junk chinoiserie and coy pastoral scenes,

you too were a kind of artist, a rage-for-order freak
setting against a man's aesthetic of cars and golf
your ornaments and other breakable stuff.
Visible from your window the sixth-century
abbey church of Colum and Malachi,
'light of the world' once in the monastic ages,
home of antiphonary and the radiant pages
of shining scripture; though you had your own
idea of the beautiful, not unrelated to Tolstoy
but formed in a tough city of ships and linen,
Harland & Wolff, Mackie's, Gallaher's, Lyle & Kinahan
and your own York St. Flax Spinning Co. Ltd.,
where you worked with a thousand others before the war;
of trams and shopping arcades, dance-hall and 'milk bar',
cold picnics at Whitehead and Donaghadee,
of Henry Joy McCracken and Wolfe Tone,
a glimmer of hope indefinitely postponed,
daft musicals at the Curzon and the Savoy;
later, a bombing raid glimpsed from your bedroom window,
utility clothing, US armoured divisions here,
the dwindling industries. (Where now the great
liners that raised their bows at the end of the street?
Ophidian shapes among the chandeliers,
wood-boring organisms at the swirling stairs.)
Beneath a Castilian sky, at a great mystic's rococo tomb,
I thought of the plain Protestant fatalism of home.
Remember 1690; prepare to meet thy God.
I grew up among washing-lines and grey skies,
pictures of Brookeborough on the gable-ends,
revolvers, RUC, B-Specials, law-'n'-order,
a hum of drums above the summer glens
echoing like *Götterdämmerung* over lough water
in a violent post-industrial sunset blaze
while you innocently hummed 'South of the Border',
'On a Slow Boat to China', 'Beyond the Blue Horizon'.

. . . Little soul, the body's guest and companion,
this is a cold epitaph from your only son,
the wish genuine if the tone ambiguous.
Oh, I can love you now that you're dead and gone
to the many mansions in your mother's house.
All artifice stripped away, we give you back to nature
but something of you, perhaps the incurable ache
of art, goes with me as I travel south
past misty drumlins, shining lanes to the shore,
above the Mournes a final helicopter,
sun-showers and rainbows all the way through Louth,
cottages buried deep in ivy and rhododendron,
ranch houses, dusty palms, blue skies of the republic . . .

XIX

On the Automation of the Irish Lights

He could see windows in it; he could even see washing
spread on the rocks to dry.

— Virginia Woolf,
To the Lighthouse

We go to the lighthouse over a golf-course now,
not whins and heather as we used to do,
though we loved golf a generation ago
when it was old sticks and rain-sodden sand —
the sea breeze and first-morning-springy turf,
the dewy, liminal silence of the rough,
the little club-house with its tin roof,
steamers and lightships half a mile from land,
an old sea civilization; but now, unmanned,
the wave-washed granite and limestone towers stand
on the edge of space untouched by human hand,
a routine enlightenment, bright but abandoned.
So long from Alexandria to Fastnet and Hawaii,
to Rathlin, Baily, Kinsale, Mizen, Cape Clear.
These are the stars in the mud, the moth's desire,
the cosmic golf that guides us *ab aeterno*
to 'a little cottage with a light in the window';
like Ptolemy and Ussher the mind creates
its own universe with these co-ordinates
marked out by beacons of perpetual fire
from the centuries of monastic candle-power
to the new technologies and the solar glow —
we are star water; as above, below.
Think (i) of evening light and tower shadow,
the families living in the toy buildings there
beneath that generalized, impartial stare,
the children 'abstract, neutral and austere',

star-clustering summer dusk, a single bird;
and (ii) rock keepers. Imagine them off-shore
in their world of siren-song, kelpie and mermaid,
listening to the wind and short-wave radio
and exercising as best they can in tiny
gardens above the sea. Think finally (iii)
of tower lights rising sheer out of the sea
where after gales the grumbling boulder knocks,
shaking the whole place, at igneous rocks.
Wind high among stars, solstice and equinox
will come and go unnoticed by human eye —
no more solitude, dark nights of the soul,
we lose singularity in excess of illumination;
the new noisy learning replaces the midnight oil,
the lonely garret and the silence of the Sorbonne.
Now the ivory towers will be 'visitor centres'
visited mostly during the long winters
by sea-birds — cormorant, puffin, kittiwake —
and their quartz lenses' own impersonal stroke
while automatically their hard gem-like flames
circulating at night unseen in empty rooms
preside over global warming and polar melt-down,
over Bill Long's *Marie-Céleste* effect and 'sonar-singing dark'.

XX

Christmas in Kinsale

> *Beyond the branches he saw the roof of her hut shining*
> *against the galactic spawn.*
> — Aidan Higgins, *Flotsam and Jetsam*

After the fairy lights in seaside lounge and bar
the night walk under a blustery Advent sky,
sidereal frost systems money will never buy,
one gull on a night wave, one polished star,
crane-light at the quayside, a dark harbour-mouth.
Stars in the spars, Spar closing, Quinnsworth
and Super Valu shut, the oracles are dumb,
the blow-ins drinking for the thirst to come
on the estuary we swam once like the Bosphorus,
moonlight on ripples like flecks of phosphorus,
pausing at mid-stream to watch stars burn,
wild gas we transit, the crushed dirt and ice,
a heavenly multitude, rock-storms of space,
methane of Jupiter, the rings of Saturn —
already rock stars have their names up there,
ashes in post-obituary orbit for eternity.
The young are slouching into Bethlehem
as zealots turn out for the millennium
on Sinai and Everest, Patmos and Ararat,
container bodies, gaze fixed on the night
for a roaring wind and the promised meteorite
of fire and brimstone; Druid and Jacobite
will be there watching for the swords of light,
the *aisling* and the dreamt apocalypse
between an earthquake and a solar eclipse.
. . . Wind-chimes this morning as in younger years
from the Church of Ireland and the Carmelite friars,
smoke rising like incense from a chimney-pot.

56

Once, angels on every branch, scribes in the trees,
'a continuous chorus of divine praise'.
Does history, exhausted, come full cycle?
It ended here at a previous *fin de siècle*
though leaving vestiges of a distant past
before Elizabeth and the Tudor conquest —
since when, four hundred years of solitude,
rainfall on bluebells in an autumn wood . . .
Holed up here in the cold gardens of the west
I take out at mid-morning my Christmas rubbish.
Sphere-music, the morning stars consort together
in a fine blaze of anticyclone weather
hallowing the calm inner and the rough outer harbour,
the silence of frost and crow on telephone lines,
the wet and dry, the garbage and the trash,
remains of rib and chop, warm cinders, ash,
bags, boxes, bulbs and batteries, bathroom waste,
carcases, tinfoil, leaves, crumbs, scraps and bones —
if this were summer there would be clouds of flies
buzzing for joy around the rubbish bins.
The harsh will dies here among snails and peonies,
its grave an iridescence in the sea-breeze,
a bucket of water where the rainbow ends.
Elsewhere the cutting edge, the tough cities,
the nuclear wind from Windscale, derelict zones;
here the triumph of carnival, rinds and skins,
mud-wrestling organisms in post-historical phase
and the fuzzy vegetable glow of origins.
A cock crows good-morning from an oil-drum
like a peacock on a rain-barrel in Byzantium,
soap-bubbles foam in a drainpipe and life begins.
I dreamed last night of a blue Cycladic dawn,
a lone figure pointing to the horizon,
again the white islands shouting, 'Come on; come on!' . . .